57818478

E306.85
HOR

Everyone Visits
Family

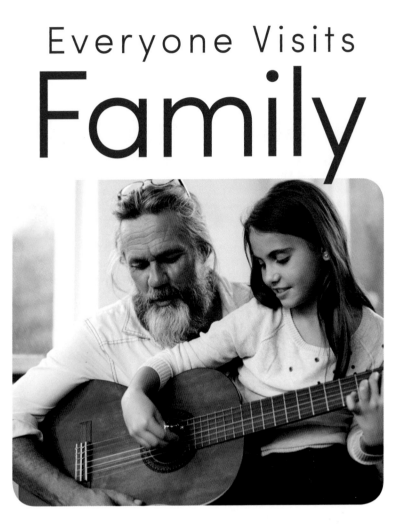

Colleen Hord

Educational Media

rourkeeducationalmedia.com

Teaching Focus:

Contractions- Find the contraction used in the book and write it down. Write the two words that make up this contraction underneath it. How are they the same? What letters are missing? What other contractions do you know?

Before Reading:

Building Academic Vocabulary and Background Knowledge

Before reading a book, it is important to set the stage for your child or student by using pre-reading strategies. This will help them develop their vocabulary, increase their reading comprehension, and make connections across the curriculum.

1. *Read the title and look at the cover. Let's make predictions about what this book will be about.*
2. *Take a picture walk by talking about the pictures/photographs in the book. Implant the vocabulary as you take the picture walk. Be sure to talk about the text features such as headings, Table of Contents, glossary, bolded words, captions, charts/diagrams, or Index.*
3. *Have students read the first page of text with you then have students read the remaining text.*
4. *Strategy Talk – use to assist students while reading.*
   - *Get your mouth ready*
   - *Look at the picture*
   - *Think…does it make sense*
   - *Think…does it look right*
   - *Think…does it sound right*
   - *Chunk it – by looking for a part you know*
5. *Read it again.*
6. *After reading the book complete the activities below.*

Content Area Vocabulary
Use glossary words in a sentence.

celebrations
extended family
generations
relatives
reunion
technology

After Reading:

Comprehension and Extension Activity

After reading the book, work on the following questions with your child or students in order to check their level of reading comprehension and content mastery.

1. *Are only people who are related to you considered to be in your family? Explain. (Text to self connection)*
2. *When do people visit family? (Summarize)*
3. *Why is it important to be around family? (Asking questions)*
4. *Do you live with or nearby your extended family? (Text to self connection)*

Extension Activity

Knowing where you came from is an important part of being in a family. Ask an adult family member to help you create your family tree. Try to go back at least three generations. Make sure to put where each family member lived. You can create your family tree on plain paper or by creating a tree background. Where did your family come from? How far back could you go?

People all over the world enjoy visiting with their families.

In Cuba and Argentina, several **generations** of family members may live together.

This is called an **extended family.**

Extended families are also common in the

Middle East and Asia.

Extended families don't have to leave home to visit. They can visit at mealtime, before bedtime, or even while doing chores.

Some people live close to their grandparents, aunts, or uncles. They can walk, bike, or take a short car ride to visit anytime.

Families in Africa may live near each other in the same village.

When families can't live near each other,

they may plan special times to get together.

This is called a family **reunion**.

At reunions, **relatives** share family stories, play games, eat favorite foods, and take pictures.

Sometimes families visit at special **celebrations.**

Weddings often bring families together. In Japan, a wedding celebration may include only family members.

Families also visit during holidays and birthdays. In Mexico, families gather to honor loved ones on the Day of the Dead.

In Central and South America, families
gather for a Quinceanera to celebrate a
girl's 15th birthday.

Many people in the United States and around the world visit family members to celebrate Christmas.

In Germany, a pickle is hidden in the Christmas tree. The first child to find it gets a special gift.

Doro Wat

In Ethiopia, families gather to celebrate Enkutatash, the first day of the New Year. They share a traditional meal of flatbread and stew.

In the United States, families often gather to celebrate Thanksgiving with a feast of turkey, vegetables, and pie.

When they can't be together, some families use **technology** to visit.

Whether you live in the same house with your family or far away, visiting helps keep families connected.

Photo Glossary

 **celebrations** (sel-uh-BRAY-shuhnz): Joyous ceremonies or gatherings to mark a special event.

 **extended family** (ek-STEND-id FAM-uh-lee): A family including grandparents, aunts, uncles, and other relatives, who all live nearby or in one household.

 **generations** (jen-uh-RAY-shuhnz): A group of people who were born within a certain period of time.

relatives (REL-uh-tivz): People who are members of your family.

reunion (ree-YOON-yuhn): A meeting between people who haven't seen each other for a long time.

technology (tek-NOL-uh-jee): The use of science and engineering inventions that help solve problems and makes life easier.

Index

Websites to Visit

http://kids.usa.gov/social-studies/index.shtml

www.exploreandmore.org/world/default.htm

www.kids.nationalgeographic.com

About the Author

Colleen Hord is an elementary teacher. She lives on six acres with her husband, chickens, ducks, and peacocks. Writer's Workshop is her favorite part of her teaching day. When she isn't teaching or writing, she enjoys kayaking, walking on the beach, and visiting with her family.

Meet The Author!
www.meetREMauthors.com

Show What You Know

1. What do you do when you visit with your family members?
2. How would your life be different if you couldn't visit with your family?
3. How is visiting the same for all families no matter where they live?

www.rourkeeducationalmedia.com

PHOTO CREDITS: Cover: © Christopher Futcher, Blend Images; Title Page: © Yuri Arcurs; Page 3: © Vikram Raghuvanshi; Page 4–5: © Monkey Business Images; Page 6: © People Images; Page 7: © XiXinXing; Page 8: © Mark Bowden; Page 9: © agafapaperiapunta; Page 10: © Susan Chiang; Page 11: © Yuri; Page 12: © Monkey Business Images; Page 13: © cowardlion; Page 14: © sunsinger; Page 15: © Blend Images; Page 16: © People Images; Page 17: © Maria Pavlova, Dusty Pixel; Page 18: © Bartosz Hadyniak, Paula Brighton; Page 19: © Monkey Business Images; Page 20: © Yuri Arcurs; Page 21: © Monkey Business Images

Edited by: Keli Sipperley

Cover and Interior design by: Tara Raymo

Library of Congress PCN Data

Everyone Visits Family / Colleen Hord

(Little World Everyone Everywhere)

ISBN (hard cover)(alk. paper) 978-1-63430-364-4

ISBN (soft cover) 978-1-63430-464-1

ISBN (e-Book) 978-1-63430-561-7

Library of Congress Control Number: 2015931701

Printed in the United States of America, North Mankato, Minnesota

Also Available as:

ROURKE'S e-Books